# Rahul Gandhi: The Untold Story

Swatantra Bahadur

Published by Swatantra Bahadur, 2023.

RAHUL GANDHI: THE UNTOLD STORY

**First edition. August 24, 2023.**

ISBN: 979-8223699255

Written by Swatantra Bahadur.

# Disclaimer

The information presented in this book is intended for general informational purposes only and should not be relied upon as a substitute for professional advice or judgment. The author and publisher are not responsible for any action taken by readers based on the information provided in this book. Readers should seek appropriate professional advice or conduct their own research before making decisions related to the topics discussed in this book. The views expressed in this book are those of the author and do not necessarily reflect the views of the publisher.

# Content

I. Introduction

- Brief history of Rahul Gandhi and his political career
- The purpose of the book

II. Early Life and Education

- Family background and upbringing

- Childhood in New Delhi

- Undergraduate education at Harvard University

- Work experience at various financial and consulting firms

- Role in the family business and social work activities

- Political awakening and entry into politics

- Relationship with his mother, Sonia Gandhi, and the Gandhi-Nehru family legacy

- Personal interests and hobbies, such as reading and travel.

- Educational background and early interests

III. Political Career

- Entry into politics and early years

- The role of Rahul Gandhi in building alliances and coalitions with other political parties

- Rahul Gandhi's approach to tackling corruption and promoting good governance in India

- The impact of Rahul Gandhi's leadership on the Congress party's electoral performance

- Rahul Gandhi's efforts to engage young people in politics and promote their participation in the political process

- The role of Rahul Gandhi in addressing issues such as unemployment, rural development, and healthcare in India

- Rahul Gandhi's views on foreign policy and India's role in the global community

- The challenges faced by Rahul Gandhi in political leadership and his strategies to overcome them

- The legacy of the Gandhi-Nehru family in Indian politics and Rahul Gandhi's efforts to continue their tradition of service to the people of India.

- Election to the Lok Sabha and his work as an MP

- Rise to prominence within the Congress party

- Controversies and setbacks

- Identify the challenges and opportunities facing Rahul Gandhi in his political future

IV. Ideology and Vision

- Rahul Gandhi's political ideology and vision for India

- Rahul Gandhi's vision for inclusive growth in India

- The role of social justice in Rahul Gandhi's ideology

- Rahul Gandhi's approach to economic reform and development

- The importance of youth leadership in Rahul Gandhi's vision for India

- Rahul Gandhi's views on foreign policy and India's role in the global community

- Rahul Gandhi's vision for a more transparent and accountable government in India

- The role of technology in promoting good governance in Rahul Gandhi's approach

- Rahul Gandhi's emphasis on environmental sustainability and climate action

- The importance of promoting democracy and human rights in Rahul Gandhi's ideology

- The legacy of the Gandhi-Nehru family and its influence on Rahul Gandhi's ideology and vision for India

- Key policy positions and initiatives

- Critiques and challenges to his vision

V. Rahul Gandhi and the Congress Party

- Rahul Gandhi's role within the Congress party

- Rahul Gandhi was elected president of the Indian National Congress party in December 2017, succeeding his mother Sonia Gandhi.

- The Indian National Congress party is one of the two major political parties in India, along with the Bharatiya Janata Party

(BJP). The party was founded in 1885 and played a key role in India's struggle for independence against British rule.

● The Congress party has governed India for a total of 54 years since independence in 1947, including under the leadership of Jawaharlal Nehru, Indira Gandhi, and Rajiv Gandhi.

● The party has been associated with the promotion of secularism, social democracy, and economic liberalization in India.

● The Congress party has faced criticism in recent years for alleged corruption and a decline in electoral support, particularly in the 2014 and 2019 general elections. However, it continues to be a major political force in India.

● Interactions with other party members and leaders

● Controversies and challenges within the Congress party

● Understand the political philosophy and vision of Rahul Gandhi

VI. Rahul Gandhi and Indian Politics

● The impact of Rahul Gandhi on Indian politics

● Rahul Gandhi is a member of the Indian National Congress party and has been involved in Indian politics for over a decade. He was elected to the Lok Sabha, the lower house of the Indian Parliament, for the first time in 2004.

● Rahul Gandhi has been a vocal critic of the policies of the ruling Bharatiya Janata Party (BJP), particularly on issues such as demonetization and the implementation of the Goods and Services Tax (GST).

- Rahul Gandhi has also been involved in several social and developmental initiatives, such as the Rajiv Gandhi Foundation and the National Students Union of India.

- Rahul Gandhi is known for his efforts to connect with young people and bring them into the political process. He has been involved in several initiatives aimed at engaging young people and promoting their participation in politics.

- Despite the criticism, Rahul Gandhi remains a prominent figure in Indian politics and is likely to continue to play an influential role in the future.

- The challenges and opportunities for his political future

- The broader implications of Rahul Gandhi's political philosophy and vision

VII. Conclusion

- Summary of key themes and takeaways

- Reflections on the significance of Rahul Gandhi for Indian politics

- Possible future directions for research on Rahul Gandhi and his impact on Indian politics

# I. Introduction

Rahul Gandhi is one of the most important and intriguing figures in Indian politics today. Born into the Nehru-Gandhi family, he has been a member of the Indian National Congress since 2004, and has held various positions within the party over the years. Despite facing many setbacks and controversies, he has emerged as a key electoral force and a significant voice within the Congress party and Indian politics more broadly.

This book aims to provide a comprehensive overview of Rahul Gandhi's life, career, and political vision. It explores his upbringing and education, his rise to prominence within the Congress party, his policy positions and initiatives, and his impact on Indian politics. Drawing on a range of sources and perspectives, this book seeks to provide a balanced and nuanced portrait of Rahul Gandhi, his strengths and weaknesses, and his potential future trajectory.

Through this book, readers will gain a greater understanding of Rahul Gandhi and his contribution to Indian politics, as well as the broader political and social context in which he operates. Whether you are a student of Indian politics, a general reader interested in the topic, or simply curious about Rahul Gandhi and his ideas, this book is sure to provide valuable insights and perspectives.

# 1. Brief history of Rahul Gandhi and his political career

Rahul Gandhi was born on June 19, 1970, in Delhi, India. He is the son of Rajiv Gandhi, who served as the Prime Minister of India from 1984 to 1989, and Sonia Gandhi, who is the current president of the Indian National Congress.

Rahul Gandhi's entry into politics began in 2004, when he contested and won his first Lok Sabha election from the constituency of Amethi in Uttar Pradesh. Over the years, he has held various positions within the Congress party, serving as the General Secretary in charge of the Indian Youth Congress and the National Students Union of India, and later as the Vice President and President of the Indian National Congress.

Throughout his political career, Rahul Gandhi has faced both praise and criticism. Supporters see him as a charismatic and dynamic leader who can connect with the youth and working class of India. Detractors, on the other hand, criticize him for his perceived lack of experience and hesitancy in making bold policy decisions.

Despite the controversies and setbacks, Rahul Gandhi remains a key electoral force and a significant voice within the Congress party. His ideas and policy positions have helped shape the political discourse in India, and his contribution to Indian politics continues to be widely debated and discussed.

# 2. The purpose of the book

The purpose of this book is to provide a comprehensive and objective overview of Rahul Gandhi's life, career, and political vision. The book aims to explore his upbringing and education, his rise to prominence within the Congress party, his policy positions and initiatives, and his impact on Indian politics.

Through this book, readers will gain a deeper understanding of Rahul Gandhi's personal and political journey, as well as his contributions to Indian politics. The book will provide an in-depth analysis of his policy positions and initiatives, and explore the controversies and challenges he has faced throughout his career.

This book is intended for a wide range of readers interested in Indian politics, including students, academics, journalists, and anyone interested in learning more about Rahul Gandhi and his ideas. The ultimate goal of the book is to provide a balanced and nuanced portrait of Rahul Gandhi, his strengths and weaknesses, and his potential future trajectory.

# II. Early Life and Education

Rahul Gandhi was born on June 19, 1970, in Delhi, India. He was the first of two children born to Rajiv Gandhi and Sonia Gandhi. His paternal grandparents were former Prime Ministers of India, Jawaharlal Nehru and Indira Gandhi, and his maternal grandfather was an Italian businessman, Stefano Maino.

Growing up, Rahul Gandhi spent much of his childhood in New Delhi and attended the Modern School. At the age of 18, he moved to the United States to attend Harvard University, where he earned a Bachelor of Arts degree in 1994. After Harvard, he worked in London for a consulting firm before returning to India in the early 2000s to pursue a career in politics.

Rahul Gandhi's education and upbringing have given him a unique perspective on Indian politics. As a member of the Nehru-Gandhi family, he has been exposed to the inner workings of Indian politics from an early age. His education in the United States has also given him a global perspective on political and social issues, which has helped to shape his policy positions and vision for India.

# 1. Family background and upbringing

Rahul Gandhi was born into one of India's most prominent political families. His father, Rajiv Gandhi, served as the Prime Minister of India from 1984 to 1989, before being assassinated in 1991. His mother, Sonia Gandhi, is the current president of the Indian National Congress.

Rahul Gandhi's paternal grandfather, Jawaharlal Nehru, was India's first Prime Minister and a key figure in the Indian independence movement. His maternal grandmother, Indira Gandhi, served as the Prime Minister of India from 1966 to 1977 and again from 1980 to 1984, until she was assassinated by her own bodyguards.

Growing up, Rahul Gandhi was exposed to the inner workings of Indian politics from an early age. He accompanied his parents on many political trips and was schooled in the importance of public service and social justice. Despite his privileged background, he was taught the importance of humility and service to others.

In addition to his family background, Rahul Gandhi's upbringing has also influenced his political philosophy. He has spoken about the importance of empowering marginalized communities and ensuring equal opportunities for all, regardless of caste, class, or religion. He has also been influenced by the teachings of Mahatma Gandhi and Martin Luther King Jr., who emphasized the importance of non-violent resistance and social justice.

# 2. Childhood in New Delhi

Rahul Gandhi spent his childhood in New Delhi, the capital city of India. He was born on June 19, 1970, in New Delhi, and grew up in a family that was deeply involved in Indian politics. His father, Rajiv Gandhi, served as the Prime Minister of India from 1984 to 1989, and his mother, Sonia Gandhi, has been the President of the Indian National Congress, India's oldest political party.

During his childhood, Rahul Gandhi attended some of the most prestigious schools in India, including St. Columba's School and The Doon School. He was known for being a quiet and introverted child, and was often described as being shy and reserved. However, he was also known for being a diligent student and for his passion for reading, which he developed at an early age.

As a child, Rahul Gandhi was exposed to the world of Indian politics and was often seen accompanying his parents to political rallies and events. His family's involvement in politics had a significant impact on his upbringing and his eventual decision to enter politics himself. Despite his father's assassination in 1991, Rahul Gandhi continued to be involved in politics and has since become a prominent political figure in India.

# 3. Undergraduate education at Harvard University

Rahul Gandhi pursued his undergraduate education at Harvard University, one of the most prestigious universities in the world. After completing his schooling in India, he moved to the United States to attend Harvard, where he earned a Bachelor's degree in 1994.

At Harvard, Rahul Gandhi studied a wide range of subjects, including economics, political science, and international relations. He was known for being an excellent student and was often praised by his professors for his intelligence and dedication to his studies. During his time at Harvard, he also developed an interest in public service and social justice, which would later become a central focus of his political career in India.

Rahul Gandhi's education at Harvard had a significant impact on his personal and professional development, and helped to shape his political vision and values. He was exposed to a diverse range of ideas and perspectives, and was able to develop a deeper understanding of global issues and challenges. His time at Harvard also gave him the skills and knowledge needed to become a successful and effective political leader in India, and he has since used his education and experience to promote social justice, economic equality, and democratic values in India.

# 4. Work experience at various financial and consulting firms

After completing his undergraduate education at Harvard University, Rahul Gandhi gained work experience at various financial and consulting firms in London and Mumbai. He worked as a management consultant at the London-based strategy consulting firm, Monitor Group, where he advised companies on business strategy and management.

Later, he worked in Mumbai as a consultant with the management consulting firm, the Monitor Group's Indian branch. He also worked with the consulting firm, Backops Services Private Ltd, where he helped to develop the company's business strategy and operations.

Rahul Gandhi's work experience in the private sector gave him valuable insights into the workings of the business world and helped him to develop skills and knowledge that would later prove useful in his political career. His experience in consulting and strategy also helped him to develop a strong analytical and problem-solving skills, which he has since used to tackle some of India's most pressing social and economic challenges.

Despite his success in the private sector, Rahul Gandhi eventually decided to enter politics and to use his skills and experience to promote social justice and democratic values in India. His work experience in the private sector has helped him to understand the needs and aspirations of India's growing middle class, and has given him a unique perspective on how to promote economic growth and development in a way that is both sustainable and inclusive.

# 5. Role in the family business and social work activities

Rahul Gandhi is a member of the influential Gandhi family and has played a significant role in the family business and social work activities. The Gandhi family owns a number of businesses, including a publishing house and a newspaper, and Rahul Gandhi has been involved in managing these businesses, along with other members of his family.

In addition to his involvement in the family business, Rahul Gandhi has also been involved in a number of social work activities. He has been an active participant in the National Rural Health Mission, a government-led initiative aimed at improving healthcare in rural areas of India. He has also been involved in efforts to improve access to education and healthcare for marginalized communities in India.

One of Rahul Gandhi's most notable social work initiatives has been the Rajiv Gandhi Foundation, a non-profit organization established in memory of his father, Rajiv Gandhi. The foundation works to promote social and economic development in India, with a focus on education, healthcare, and rural development. Rahul Gandhi has been actively involved in the foundation's work, serving as its Vice Chairman and promoting its initiatives across India.

Overall, Rahul Gandhi's involvement in the family business and social work activities has helped him to develop a deep understanding of the needs and aspirations of people across India. His focus on social justice and economic equality has been shaped by his experiences working with marginalized communities and promoting development initiatives across India.

# 6. Political awakening and entry into politics

Rahul Gandhi's political awakening and entry into politics was heavily influenced by the assassination of his father, Rajiv Gandhi, in 1991. Following his father's death, Rahul Gandhi spent several years in the private sector, working in finance and consulting, before deciding to enter politics in 2004.

Rahul Gandhi's decision to enter politics was driven by a desire to continue his family's legacy of service to the people of India. He joined the Indian National Congress, India's oldest political party, and was soon appointed as the General Secretary of the party. In this role, he worked to revitalize the Congress party and to promote its message of social justice and economic equality.

In 2007, Rahul Gandhi was appointed as the Chairman of the Indian Youth Congress, the youth wing of the Congress party. In this role, he worked to engage young people in politics and to promote their participation in the political process. He also focused on issues such as education, employment, and healthcare, which are of particular importance to young people in India.

Over the years, Rahul Gandhi has played an increasingly prominent role in Indian politics, serving as a Member of Parliament from Amethi constituency in Uttar Pradesh. He has also served as the Vice President and later, President of the Indian National Congress. In these roles, he has worked to promote the Congress party's message of social justice, economic equality, and democratic values.

Overall, Rahul Gandhi's entry into politics was driven by a desire to continue his family's legacy of service to the people of India and to promote a more equitable and just society. His focus on engaging young people in politics and promoting their participation in the political process has helped to create a new generation of leaders in India.

# 7. Relationship with his mother, Sonia Gandhi, and the Gandhi-Nehru family legacy

Rahul Gandhi has had a close and supportive relationship with his mother, Sonia Gandhi, throughout his life and political career. Sonia Gandhi has played a significant role in the Indian National Congress party, serving as its President for many years and helping to shape its policies and vision. She has also been a guiding force for Rahul Gandhi, providing him with advice and support as he has navigated the often-challenging landscape of Indian politics.

The Gandhi-Nehru family legacy has been a central part of Rahul Gandhi's life and political career. He comes from a family with a long and illustrious history in Indian politics, with several of his family members serving as Prime Ministers of India. This legacy has had a significant impact on his upbringing and his political vision and values.

Rahul Gandhi has often spoken about the importance of continuing his family's legacy of service to the people of India and promoting social justice, economic equality, and democratic values. He has also emphasized the need to adapt to changing times and to address new challenges facing India in the 21st century.

Overall, Rahul Gandhi's relationship with his mother, Sonia Gandhi, and his family's legacy in Indian politics have played a significant role in shaping his political career and vision. He has worked to continue his family's tradition of serving the people of India and promoting social and economic justice, while also charting a new course for the Congress party and Indian politics in the modern era.

# 8. Personal interests and hobbies, such as reading and travel.

Rahul Gandhi has a variety of personal interests and hobbies, including reading and travel. He has been an avid reader from a young age and his passion for reading has continued throughout his life. He enjoys reading books on a wide range of topics, including history, politics, and philosophy, among others.

Travel is another passion of Rahul Gandhi. He has traveled extensively across India and the world, visiting different countries and learning about their cultures and traditions. In particular, he is interested in exploring the ways in which different societies and cultures have developed and evolved over time.

Apart from reading and travel, Rahul Gandhi is also interested in sports, particularly cricket. He is a fan of the Indian cricket team and has been known to attend matches and support the team.

Overall, Rahul Gandhi's interests and hobbies reflect his curiosity and passion for learning about the world around him. His love for reading and travel has helped him to develop a broad perspective on global issues and challenges, while his interest in sports has given him a way to connect with the people of India and to promote a sense of national pride and unity.

# 9. Educational background and early interests

Rahul Gandhi's educational background and early interests have played a significant role in shaping his political views and career. After completing his schooling at the Modern School in New Delhi, he went on to attend St. Stephen's College at the University of Delhi, where he earned a Bachelor of Arts degree in 1989. He then went on to study at Harvard University in the United States, where he earned a Bachelor of Arts degree in 1994.

During his time at Harvard, Rahul Gandhi became interested in global issues and social justice. He spent a summer in London working for a consulting firm, and later worked for a management firm in Mumbai before entering full-time politics. His education in the United States and exposure to different cultures and viewpoints have given him a broader perspective on Indian politics, and have influenced his policy positions on issues such as education, healthcare, and poverty alleviation.

Early in his political career, Rahul Gandhi focused on youth issues and worked to promote the empowerment of young people in India. He became the General Secretary of the Indian Youth Congress in 2007 and later the National Students Union of India, where he worked to increase youth participation in Indian politics. His early interests in youth empowerment and social justice have continued to shape his political views and policy positions throughout his career.

# III. Political Career

Rahul Gandhi's political career began in earnest in 2004, when he contested the Lok Sabha elections from the constituency of Amethi in Uttar Pradesh. Despite his relative lack of political experience, he won the election by a wide margin, and has since been re-elected from the same constituency in several subsequent elections.

Over the years, Rahul Gandhi has held various positions within the Indian National Congress, including serving as the General Secretary for the Indian Youth Congress and the National Students Union of India. He later served as the Vice President of the Congress party from 2013 to 2017, and then as its President from 2017 to 2019.

Throughout his political career, Rahul Gandhi has been known for his focus on issues such as poverty alleviation, education, and healthcare. He has taken a particular interest in empowering marginalized communities, and has advocated for policies that prioritize their needs and concerns. He has also been a vocal proponent of environmental protection and has spoken out against climate change.

Despite his many accomplishments, Rahul Gandhi has also faced criticism and controversy throughout his political career. His perceived lack of experience and hesitancy in making bold policy decisions have led some to question his leadership abilities. Additionally, his handling of certain scandals and controversies has drawn criticism from some quarters.

Nevertheless, Rahul Gandhi remains a key figure in Indian politics and a significant voice within the Congress party. His ideas and policy positions continue to shape the political discourse in India, and his contribution to Indian politics is widely debated and discussed.

# 1. Entry into politics and early years

Rahul Gandhi's entry into politics began in 2004 when he contested the Lok Sabha elections from the constituency of Amethi in Uttar Pradesh. Despite initial skepticism about his political abilities, he won the election by a wide margin, and has since been re-elected to the same constituency in several subsequent elections.

In his early years as a Member of Parliament, Rahul Gandhi focused on youth issues and worked to promote the empowerment of young people in India. He became the General Secretary of the Indian Youth Congress in 2007 and later the National Students Union of India, where he worked to increase youth participation in Indian politics.

Over the years, Rahul Gandhi has been involved in various developmental projects in his constituency, including the establishment of schools, hospitals, and other infrastructure. He has also been a vocal proponent of environmental protection and has spoken out against climate change.

In 2013, Rahul Gandhi was appointed as the Vice President of the Indian National Congress, and was seen as the de facto successor to his mother, Sonia Gandhi, who was then the party's president. In this role, he played a key role in the Congress party's campaign for the 2014 Lok Sabha elections, but the party suffered a crushing defeat at the hands of the Bharatiya Janata Party (BJP).

In the aftermath of the 2014 election, Rahul Gandhi faced criticism for his handling of the Congress party's campaign and was seen by many as lacking the leadership skills needed to revive the party's fortunes. However, he remained committed to his vision for India and continued to work towards empowering marginalized communities and promoting youth participation in politics.

Despite the challenges and setbacks, Rahul Gandhi remains a key figure in Indian politics and a significant voice within the Congress party. His ideas and policy positions continue to shape the political discourse in India, and his contribution to Indian politics is widely debated and discussed.

# 2. The role of Rahul Gandhi in building alliances and coalitions with other political parties

Rahul Gandhi has played a key role in building alliances and coalitions with other political parties in India. He recognizes that no single party can address all of the complex issues facing India and that political cooperation is essential for creating meaningful change.

One of Rahul Gandhi's most significant efforts in this regard was the formation of the United Progressive Alliance (UPA) in 2004. The UPA was a coalition of several political parties, including the Indian National Congress, that came together to oppose the ruling Bharatiya Janata Party (BJP) and to promote a more inclusive and equitable vision of India. The UPA was successful in winning the 2004 and 2009 general elections and formed the government of India for 10 years.

In addition to the UPA, Rahul Gandhi has also worked to build alliances with other regional and state-based political parties. For example, in the 2017 Uttar Pradesh State Assembly elections, he formed an alliance with the Samajwadi Party. This alliance was successful in winning a significant number of seats in the state assembly.

Rahul Gandhi's approach to building alliances is based on the idea of creating a broad-based coalition that represents the diverse interests and perspectives of the Indian people. He believes that political cooperation across parties and ideologies is essential for promoting social justice, economic equality, and democratic values in India.

Overall, Rahul Gandhi's efforts to build alliances and coalitions with other political parties reflect his commitment to creating a more inclusive and equitable India. His vision for political cooperation across parties and regions is an important step towards building a more unified and prosperous India.

# 3. Rahul Gandhi's approach to tackling corruption and promoting good governance in India

Rahul Gandhi has consistently emphasized the need to tackle corruption and promote good governance in India. He believes that corruption undermines democracy and erodes the public trust in government institutions, and that it is essential to root out corruption in order to create a more transparent and accountable government.

One of Rahul Gandhi's key strategies for tackling corruption is to promote transparency and accountability in government institutions. He supports measures such as the Right to Information Act, which gives citizens the right to access information from government institutions, and the Lokpal Bill, which creates an independent ombudsman to investigate cases of corruption.

Rahul Gandhi has also called for greater political and electoral reforms to promote good governance in India. He has emphasized the need to reduce the influence of money and power in politics and to create a more level playing field for all political parties.

Another approach Rahul Gandhi has taken to combat corruption is by promoting the use of technology in government institutions. He believes that technology can help to create a more transparent and accountable government by reducing opportunities for corruption and improving the efficiency of government services.

Overall, Rahul Gandhi's approach to tackling corruption and promoting good governance in India is focused on creating a more transparent, accountable, and efficient government. He recognizes that this is a long-term effort and that it requires the active participation of citizens, civil society organizations, and government institutions.

# 4. The impact of Rahul Gandhi's leadership on the Congress party's electoral performance

Rahul Gandhi has had a significant impact on the electoral performance of the Indian National Congress party during his leadership tenure. While the Congress party has faced challenges in recent years, Rahul Gandhi's leadership has helped to revitalize the party and to reconnect with voters across India.

One of Rahul Gandhi's key strategies has been to engage with young people and to promote their participation in the political process. He has been successful in drawing a large number of young people into the Congress party and has emphasized the importance of their role in shaping the future of India.

Another important aspect of Rahul Gandhi's leadership has been his focus on social justice and economic equality. He has worked to promote policies and programs that address the needs of marginalized communities, such as farmers, women, and minorities. This focus on social justice has helped to draw support from a wide range of people across India.

Rahul Gandhi has also been instrumental in building alliances and coalitions with other political parties. These alliances have helped to broaden the Congress party's base of support and to create a more united opposition to the ruling Bharatiya Janata Party (BJP).

While the Congress party has faced challenges in recent years, including setbacks in some state elections, Rahul Gandhi's leadership has been critical in keeping the party united and focused on its core principles of social justice, economic equality, and democratic values. His vision for the future of India and his commitment to inclusive and equitable growth have resonated with a growing number of voters across the country.

# 5. Rahul Gandhi's efforts to engage young people in politics and promote their participation in the political process

Rahul Gandhi has made significant efforts to engage young people in politics and promote their participation in the political process in India. He recognizes that young people are the future of India and that their voices and perspectives are essential for building a more inclusive and equitable society.

One of the key ways in which Rahul Gandhi has engaged young people in politics is by actively reaching out to them and listening to their concerns and ideas. He has held numerous rallies and meetings with young people across India and has encouraged them to take an active role in shaping the future of the country.

Rahul Gandhi has also worked to create opportunities for young people to get involved in the political process. He has emphasized the importance of youth leadership in the Congress party and has encouraged young people to run for office and to participate in the party's decision-making processes.

Another important aspect of Rahul Gandhi's efforts to engage young people in politics has been his use of social media and technology. He has been active on social media platforms such as Twitter and Facebook and has used these platforms to connect with young people and to share his vision for the future of India.

Overall, Rahul Gandhi's efforts to engage young people in politics reflect his commitment to creating a more inclusive and participatory political system in India. His focus on youth leadership and his use of social media and technology have helped to create new opportunities for young people to get involved in the political process and to shape the future of the country.

# 6. The role of Rahul Gandhi in addressing issues such as unemployment, rural development, and healthcare in India

Rahul Gandhi has been an active proponent of policies and programs aimed at addressing some of the most pressing issues facing India, such as unemployment, rural development, and healthcare.

One of Rahul Gandhi's key priorities has been to address the issue of unemployment in India, particularly among young people. He has called for the creation of new job opportunities, particularly in the manufacturing and services sectors, and has emphasized the importance of skills training and education to prepare young people for the workforce.

Rahul Gandhi has also been a vocal advocate for rural development in India. He recognizes that a significant portion of India's population still lives in rural areas and that these communities often lack access to basic services and infrastructure. He has called for increased investment in rural infrastructure, such as roads, electricity, and water supply, as well as in agriculture and other rural industries.

In addition to these issues, Rahul Gandhi has also been a strong advocate for improving healthcare in India. He has called for increased investment in healthcare infrastructure and services, particularly in rural areas, and has emphasized the importance of universal access to healthcare for all Indians.

Overall, Rahul Gandhi's role in addressing issues such as unemployment, rural development, and healthcare reflects his commitment to promoting inclusive and equitable growth in India. He recognizes that these issues are complex and require a coordinated effort by government, civil society organizations, and the private sector to address them effectively. His vision for India is one in which all citizens have access to the opportunities and resources they need to achieve their full potential.

# 7. Rahul Gandhi's views on foreign policy and India's role in the global community

Rahul Gandhi has expressed a number of views on foreign policy and India's role in the global community. He believes that India has an important role to play in promoting peace, stability, and prosperity in the world, and that it is essential for India to engage actively with other countries and international organizations to achieve these goals.

One of Rahul Gandhi's key priorities in foreign policy is to strengthen India's relationships with its neighbors and to promote regional stability and cooperation. He has emphasized the importance of building stronger ties with countries such as China, Pakistan, and Bangladesh, and has called for greater cooperation on issues such as trade, security, and development.

Rahul Gandhi has also been a vocal advocate for India's role in the global fight against climate change. He has called for increased investment in renewable energy and for greater cooperation between India and other countries to reduce greenhouse gas emissions and mitigate the impact of climate change.

In addition, Rahul Gandhi has emphasized the importance of promoting democracy and human rights around the world. He believes that India has a responsibility to use its influence to promote democratic values and to support efforts to protect human rights and fundamental freedoms.

Overall, Rahul Gandhi's views on foreign policy reflect his commitment to promoting a more peaceful, stable, and equitable world. He recognizes that India has a unique role to play in the global community and that it is essential for India to engage actively with other countries and international organizations to achieve its goals.

# 8. The challenges faced by Rahul Gandhi in political leadership and his strategies to overcome them

As a political leader, Rahul Gandhi has faced a number of challenges over the years. These challenges have included electoral setbacks, criticism from within and outside his party, and the need to balance the demands of his leadership role with his personal life.

One of Rahul Gandhi's main strategies for overcoming these challenges has been to remain focused on his core principles and values. He has been vocal about his commitment to social justice, economic equality, and democratic values, and has emphasized the importance of staying true to these principles even in the face of criticism or setbacks.

Another strategy that Rahul Gandhi has employed is to engage with voters and to listen to their concerns and ideas. He has been active in meeting with people across India and has emphasized the importance of taking a grassroots approach to politics.

Rahul Gandhi has also emphasized the need for political cooperation and alliances with other parties. He has worked to build alliances and coalitions with other political parties and has emphasized the importance of working together to achieve common goals.

In addition, Rahul Gandhi has used social media and technology to connect with young people and to build a broader base of support. He has been active on social media platforms such as Twitter and Facebook and has used these platforms to engage with young people and to promote his vision for the future of India.

Overall, Rahul Gandhi's strategies for overcoming the challenges of political leadership reflect his commitment to his core principles and his belief in the importance of listening to and engaging with voters. His focus on grassroots engagement, political cooperation, and the use of technology has helped to keep him connected with the changing needs and aspirations of the Indian people.

# 9. The legacy of the Gandhi-Nehru family in Indian politics and Rahul Gandhi's efforts to continue their tradition of service to the people of India.

The Gandhi-Nehru family has had a significant impact on Indian politics and history, and their legacy continues to shape the country today. Jawaharlal Nehru, India's first prime minister and a member of the family, played a critical role in India's struggle for independence and in shaping the country's political and economic policies. His daughter, Indira Gandhi, also served as prime minister and made significant contributions to India's development, especially in areas such as agriculture, education, and healthcare. Rajiv Gandhi, her son and Rahul Gandhi's father, also served as prime minister and played a key role in modernizing India's economy and infrastructure.

Rahul Gandhi has sought to continue the family's tradition of service to the people of India. He has emphasized the importance of social justice, economic equality, and democratic values, and has worked to promote policies and programs that address the needs of marginalized communities, such as farmers, women, and minorities. Rahul Gandhi's vision for India is one that is inclusive, equitable, and compassionate, and he has sought to build a political movement that is grounded in these values.

In addition to continuing the family's legacy of service, Rahul Gandhi has also sought to modernize the Congress party and to make it more responsive to the needs of the Indian people. He has emphasized the importance of youth leadership and has worked to engage young people in politics and in the party's decision-making processes.

Overall, Rahul Gandhi's efforts to continue the Gandhi-Nehru family's tradition of service to the people of India reflect his commitment to promoting a more just, equitable, and democratic society. His vision for India is one that is based on the principles of social justice, economic equality, and democratic values, and he has worked tirelessly to promote these values throughout his political career.

# 10. Election to the Lok Sabha and his work as an MP

Rahul Gandhi's entry into politics began in 2004 when he contested the Lok Sabha elections from the constituency of Amethi in Uttar Pradesh. He won the election by a wide margin, and has since been re-elected to the same constituency in several subsequent elections. As a Member of Parliament, Rahul Gandhi has focused on a variety of issues related to the development of his constituency and the welfare of its people.

Over the years, Rahul Gandhi has initiated various developmental projects in his constituency, including the establishment of schools, hospitals, and other infrastructure. He has worked to improve the standard of living of the people of Amethi and has been a vocal advocate for the rights of farmers and other marginalized communities.

As an MP, Rahul Gandhi has also been involved in various initiatives aimed at promoting youth participation in politics. He has taken a keen interest in empowering the youth of India and has worked to provide them with the resources and opportunities they need to become active and engaged citizens.

In addition to his work in Amethi, Rahul Gandhi has been involved in national politics as well. He has played a key role in shaping the Congress party's policies and has been a vocal advocate for a range of issues related to social justice and environmental protection.

Throughout his time as an MP, Rahul Gandhi has been known for his accessibility and his willingness to engage with his constituents. He has made a concerted effort to understand the needs and concerns of the people he represents and has worked tirelessly to address their issues and improve their lives.

Overall, Rahul Gandhi's work as an MP has been driven by a strong commitment to the welfare of the people he represents and to the progressive values that he holds dear. Despite the challenges and setbacks he has faced, he remains a key figure in Indian politics and a source of inspiration to many.

# 11. Rise to prominence within the Congress party

Rahul Gandhi's rise to prominence within the Congress party began in the late 2000s when he took on a more active role in the party's affairs. He was appointed as the General Secretary for the Indian Youth Congress in 2007, and later became the National Students Union of India, where he worked to increase youth participation in Indian politics.

Over the years, Rahul Gandhi has been involved in various developmental projects in his constituency, including the establishment of schools, hospitals, and other infrastructure. He has also been a vocal proponent of environmental protection and has spoken out against climate change.

In 2013, Rahul Gandhi was appointed as the Vice President of the Indian National Congress, and was seen as the de facto successor to his mother, Sonia Gandhi, who was then the party's president. In this role, he played a key role in the Congress party's campaign for the 2014 Lok Sabha elections, but the party suffered a crushing defeat at the hands of the Bharatiya Janata Party (BJP).

Despite the setbacks, Rahul Gandhi remained committed to his vision for India and continued to work towards empowering marginalized communities and promoting youth participation in politics. In 2017, he was elected as the President of the Indian National Congress, succeeding his mother, Sonia Gandhi.

Under Rahul Gandhi's leadership, the Congress party has undergone a significant transformation. He has sought to reinvigorate the party's grassroots organization and has emphasized the importance of empowering local leaders and activists. He has also been a vocal critic of the ruling BJP government's policies, particularly on issues such as economic inequality and social justice.

Although the Congress party has faced a number of electoral defeats under Rahul Gandhi's leadership, he remains a key figure in Indian politics and continues to be a significant voice within the party. His ideas and policy positions continue to shape the political discourse in India, and his contribution to Indian politics is widely debated and discussed.

# 12. Controversies and setbacks

Despite his many accomplishments, Rahul Gandhi has faced a number of controversies and setbacks throughout his political career. One of the most notable controversies occurred in 2012, when he made a comment about the Muslim community that was widely criticized as being divisive and insensitive. He was also the target of criticism over his handling of certain scandals and controversies within the Congress party.

Rahul Gandhi has also faced criticism for his perceived lack of experience and hesitancy in making bold policy decisions. His leadership of the Congress party has been marked by a series of electoral defeats, including a crushing defeat in the 2014 Lok Sabha elections. The party's performance in subsequent elections, including the 2019 Lok Sabha elections, has also been disappointing.

Despite these setbacks, Rahul Gandhi has remained committed to his vision for India and has continued to work towards empowering marginalized communities and promoting youth participation in politics. He has taken a number of steps to revitalize the Congress party, including by emphasizing the importance of grassroots organization and empowering local leaders and activists.

Overall, Rahul Gandhi's political career has been marked by both successes and setbacks. While he has faced criticism and controversy at times, his commitment to the welfare of the people he represents and to the progressive values he holds dear continues to inspire many in India and around the world.

Rahul Gandhi has faced several controversies and setbacks throughout his political career. The exact number of controversies and setbacks is difficult to quantify, as they are often a matter of interpretation and depend on various factors such as political context and media coverage. However, some of the most notable controversies and setbacks include his controversial comment about the Muslim community in 2012, criticism over his handling of certain scandals and controversies within the Congress party, and the party's poor electoral performance in several elections under his leadership.

# 13. Identify the challenges and opportunities facing Rahul Gandhi in his political future

There are several challenges and opportunities facing Rahul Gandhi in his political future in India. Here are a few examples:

Challenges:

1. Rebuilding the Congress Party: The Congress Party has faced significant electoral defeats in recent years, and rebuilding the party's electoral base will be a significant challenge for Rahul Gandhi. He must work to re-energize the party's supporters and to promote a more united and inclusive political culture within the party.

2. Overcoming Opposition: Rahul Gandhi faces significant opposition from the ruling government, which has the power and resources to marginalize and discredit him. This opposition may make it difficult for Rahul Gandhi to advance his political agenda and to gain traction among the broader Indian public.

3. Maintaining Momentum: Rahul Gandhi has made significant gains in promoting social justice, economic equality, environmental protection, and democratic values in India. However, maintaining momentum in these areas will require sustained effort and resources.

Opportunities:

1. Promoting a Progressive Agenda: Rahul Gandhi has the opportunity to continue promoting a more progressive political agenda in India, which is resonating with many young and marginalized voters. He can work to build a more inclusive and equitable society that promotes the rights and well-being of all Indians.

2. Harnessing Technology: Technology has the power to connect people and to promote greater transparency and accountability in government. Rahul Gandhi can use technology to engage with his

supporters, to promote his political vision, and to hold the government accountable for its policies and actions.

3. Building Partnerships: Rahul Gandhi can work to build partnerships with civil society organizations, NGOs, and other political parties to advance his political agenda. These partnerships can help to amplify his message and to promote greater collaboration and cooperation in addressing India's most pressing challenges.

Overall, Rahul Gandhi faces significant challenges in his political future in India. However, he also has significant opportunities to promote a more progressive and democratic political agenda in India, to use technology to engage with his supporters and to build partnerships to advance his vision for India.

Rebuilding the Congress Party:

Rebuilding the Congress Party is one of the key challenges facing Rahul Gandhi in his political future in India. The Congress Party has faced significant electoral defeats in recent years, and rebuilding the party's electoral base will require sustained effort and resources.

To rebuild the Congress Party, Rahul Gandhi can focus on the following strategies:

1. Promoting a Clear Political Vision: Rahul Gandhi can work to promote a clear and compelling political vision that resonates with the broader Indian public. He can articulate policies and initiatives that promote social justice, economic equality, environmental protection, and democratic values, and can communicate these policies in a way that is accessible and inspiring to a diverse range of voters.

2. Building a Young and Inclusive Leadership: Rahul Gandhi can work to build a young and inclusive leadership within the Congress Party that represents the diversity of Indian society. He can promote greater representation of women, Dalits, Adivasis, and religious minorities in the party's decision-making bodies, and can provide greater opportunities for young leaders to take on leadership roles within the party.

3. Engaging with the Grassroots: Rahul Gandhi can work to engage with the Congress Party's grassroots supporters and to build stronger relationships with local communities. He can hold public meetings and rallies, conduct door-to-door campaigns, and use social media to connect with his supporters and to promote greater engagement with the party's political agenda.

4. Promoting Internal Democracy: Rahul Gandhi can work to promote greater internal democracy within the Congress Party, to ensure that all voices are heard and that decision-making is transparent and accountable. He can promote greater participation in the party's decision-making processes, and can work to build a culture of constructive debate and collaboration within the party.

Overall, rebuilding the Congress Party will require a sustained and collaborative effort from Rahul Gandhi and the party's leadership. However, with a clear political vision, a young and inclusive leadership, and a commitment to engaging with the grassroots, the Congress Party can make significant gains in promoting a more progressive and democratic political agenda in India.

Maintaining Momentum:

Maintaining momentum in promoting social justice, economic equality, environmental protection, and democratic values in India is another key challenge facing Rahul Gandhi in his political future. Here are some strategies he can use to maintain momentum:

1. Continued Advocacy: Rahul Gandhi can continue to be a vocal advocate for his political vision and agenda, and to use his platform to promote policies and initiatives that promote social justice, economic equality, environmental protection, and democratic values. He can use his speeches, interviews, and social media presence to raise awareness and build momentum around these issues.

2. Collaborative Partnerships: Collaborative partnerships with civil society organizations, NGOs, and other political parties can help Rahul Gandhi to amplify his message and to promote greater collaboration and cooperation in addressing India's most pressing

challenges. He can work to build alliances with groups and individuals who share his vision for a more just and equitable India.

3. Grassroots Mobilization: Rahul Gandhi can work to mobilize grassroots supporters around his political agenda, and to build a mass movement for social change in India. He can hold public meetings and rallies, conduct door-to-door campaigns, and use social media to connect with his supporters and to promote greater engagement with his political agenda.

4. Focus on Young Voters: Rahul Gandhi can focus on engaging with young voters in India, who are increasingly interested in promoting progressive political values and are using social media to express their political opinions. He can use social media platforms like Instagram, Twitter, and Facebook to reach out to young voters and engage them in his political agenda.

Overall, maintaining momentum in promoting a more just and equitable society in India will require sustained effort and collaboration from Rahul Gandhi and his supporters. By continuing to advocate for his political vision, building collaborative partnerships, mobilizing grassroots support, and engaging with young voters, Rahul Gandhi can maintain momentum and continue to make gains in promoting social justice, economic equality, environmental protection, and democratic values in India.

# IV. Ideology and Vision

Rahul Gandhi's ideology and vision for India are anchored in a commitment to social justice, economic equality, and environmental sustainability. He believes that the government has a responsibility to ensure that all citizens have access to basic necessities such as education, healthcare, and clean water, and that the benefits of economic growth should be shared by all.

Rahul Gandhi has been a vocal advocate for marginalized communities, including farmers, laborers, and women. He has worked to empower these communities by providing them with access to education, healthcare, and other resources, and by advocating for policies that prioritize their needs and concerns.

In addition to his commitment to social justice, Rahul Gandhi has also been a vocal proponent of environmental protection. He has spoken out against climate change and has advocated for policies that promote sustainable development and reduce reliance on fossil fuels.

Overall, Rahul Gandhi's ideology and vision are rooted in a belief in the power of government to promote the common good and to create a more just and equitable society. While his ideas and policy positions have faced criticism and controversy at times, his commitment to these values continues to inspire many in India and around the world.

# 1. Rahul Gandhi's political ideology and vision for India

Rahul Gandhi's political ideology is rooted in the principles of democracy, secularism, and social justice. He believes in a vision of India where all citizens have equal rights and opportunities, and where economic prosperity is shared by all.

One of Rahul Gandhi's key policy priorities is to reduce economic inequality and promote social justice. He is a vocal advocate for the rights of marginalized communities, including farmers, laborers, and women, and has worked to empower these communities by providing them with access to education, healthcare, and other resources. He has also supported policies that seek to reduce poverty and increase social mobility, such as the National Rural Employment Guarantee Act (NREGA).

In addition to his focus on social justice, Rahul Gandhi has also been a vocal proponent of environmental protection. He has spoken out against climate change and has advocated for policies that promote sustainable development and reduce reliance on fossil fuels.

Rahul Gandhi's vision for India also includes a strong commitment to democracy and secularism. He believes in the importance of a free and fair electoral process, and has been a vocal critic of attempts to undermine democratic institutions in India. He has also been a vocal advocate for religious tolerance and communal harmony, and has spoken out against discrimination on the basis of religion, caste, or gender.

Overall, Rahul Gandhi's political ideology and vision for India are driven by a strong commitment to social justice, economic equality, and environmental sustainability, as well as a belief in the principles of democracy and secularism. While his ideas and policy positions have faced criticism and controversy at times, his commitment to these values has earned him a significant following in India and around the world.

# 2. Rahul Gandhi's vision for inclusive growth in India

Rahul Gandhi's vision for inclusive growth in India is based on the principles of social justice, economic equality, and democratic values. He believes that economic growth must be inclusive and that all sections of society should benefit from the country's development.

One of the key elements of Rahul Gandhi's vision for inclusive growth is his commitment to reducing income and wealth inequality in India. He has called for policies and programs that prioritize the needs of the poor and marginalized communities, such as farmers, women, and minorities. Rahul Gandhi believes that economic growth should benefit everyone, not just a small elite, and that it is the responsibility of the government to ensure that the benefits of development are distributed fairly.

Rahul Gandhi also emphasizes the importance of education and skills training in promoting inclusive growth. He has called for increased investment in education and skills training to help young people acquire the skills and knowledge they need to succeed in the modern economy. Rahul Gandhi believes that education is the key to unlocking India's full potential and is essential for building a more inclusive and equitable society.

Another important aspect of Rahul Gandhi's vision for inclusive growth is his focus on creating new job opportunities. He has emphasized the importance of promoting entrepreneurship and small business development as a means of creating new jobs and reducing unemployment. Rahul Gandhi believes that a vibrant and dynamic small business sector is essential for promoting inclusive growth and reducing poverty.

Overall, Rahul Gandhi's vision for inclusive growth in India is based on the principles of social justice, economic equality, and democratic values. He believes that economic growth must be inclusive and that everyone should benefit from the country's development. Rahul Gandhi's emphasis on education, skills training, small business development, and reducing income and wealth inequality reflects his commitment to creating a more inclusive and equitable society in India.

# 3. The role of social justice in Rahul Gandhi's ideology

Social justice is a central pillar of Rahul Gandhi's ideology, and he has made it a key priority in his political career. Rahul Gandhi believes that social justice is essential for building a fair, equal, and inclusive society, and that it is the responsibility of the government to ensure that everyone has access to basic human rights and opportunities.

One of the key elements of Rahul Gandhi's approach to social justice is his emphasis on empowering marginalized communities, such as Dalits, Adivasis, and women. He has called for policies and programs that address the specific needs of these communities, such as access to education, healthcare, and employment opportunities. Rahul Gandhi believes that marginalized communities have been historically disadvantaged and that it is the responsibility of the government to provide them with equal opportunities and support.

Rahul Gandhi's approach to social justice also emphasizes the importance of promoting equal rights and opportunities for all citizens, regardless of their gender, caste, religion, or sexual orientation. He has been vocal in his support for LGBTQ rights, and has called for greater representation of women and minorities in political and economic decision-making.

Another important element of Rahul Gandhi's approach to social justice is his focus on transparency and accountability in government. He believes that corruption and nepotism are major obstacles to achieving social justice in India, and has called for greater transparency and accountability in government institutions.

Overall, Rahul Gandhi's emphasis on social justice reflects his commitment to building a more equal and inclusive society in India. He believes that social justice is not just a moral imperative, but also essential for promoting economic growth and stability. Rahul Gandhi's focus on empowering marginalized communities, promoting equal rights and opportunities, and promoting transparency and accountability in government reflects his vision for a more just, equitable, and democratic India.

# 4. Rahul Gandhi's approach to economic reform and development

Rahul Gandhi's approach to economic reform and development is based on promoting inclusive growth and creating opportunities for all sections of society to participate in the economic development of India. He believes that economic growth must be equitable and must not leave behind those who are economically marginalized.

One of the key priorities of Rahul Gandhi's economic reform agenda is job creation. He has called for policies and programs that promote entrepreneurship and small business development, which can create new job opportunities and reduce unemployment. Rahul Gandhi also emphasizes the importance of skills development and vocational training to ensure that young people are equipped with the skills they need to succeed in a rapidly changing economy.

Rahul Gandhi's approach to economic reform and development also emphasizes the importance of rural development. He believes that rural communities are often left behind in the process of economic development, and that it is essential to create opportunities for these communities to participate in the modern economy. Rahul Gandhi has called for policies and programs that promote rural infrastructure development, such as roads, electricity, and water supply, as well as increased investment in agriculture and rural industries.

Another important element of Rahul Gandhi's approach to economic reform and development is his emphasis on social welfare policies. He believes that the government has a responsibility to provide basic services and support to those who are economically disadvantaged, such as farmers, women, and minorities. Rahul Gandhi has called for policies and programs that provide access to education, healthcare, and social security to these communities.

Overall, Rahul Gandhi's approach to economic reform and development is based on promoting inclusive growth, creating job opportunities, and providing support to those who are economically marginalized. He believes that economic growth must be equitable and must not leave behind those who are most vulnerable. Rahul Gandhi's focus on rural development, social welfare policies, and skills development reflects his commitment to building a more inclusive and equitable economy in India.

# 5.The importance of youth leadership in Rahul Gandhi's vision for India

The importance of youth leadership is a key priority in Rahul Gandhi's vision for India. He has emphasized the need for young people to be actively engaged in politics and to take on leadership roles in shaping the future of the country.

Rahul Gandhi believes that young people have a unique perspective and energy that can help to drive India's growth and development. He has called for policies and programs that promote youth entrepreneurship, education, and skills development, to help young people succeed in the modern economy. Rahul Gandhi also emphasizes the importance of empowering young people to participate in decision-making processes, and has called for greater youth representation in politics and governance.

Another important element of Rahul Gandhi's approach to youth leadership is his focus on promoting gender equality. He believes that young women should have the same opportunities as young men to participate in politics and leadership roles. Rahul Gandhi has been vocal in his support for women's rights and has called for greater representation of women in political and economic decision-making.

Rahul Gandhi's emphasis on youth leadership also reflects his commitment to building a more inclusive and equitable society. He believes that young people from all backgrounds should have access to opportunities and support to succeed in their chosen field. Rahul Gandhi has called for policies and programs that address the specific needs of marginalized youth, such as those from rural communities or from economically disadvantaged backgrounds.

Overall, the importance of youth leadership is a key priority in Rahul Gandhi's vision for India. He believes that young people have a critical role to play in shaping the future of the country, and that it is essential to provide them with the support and opportunities they need to succeed. Rahul Gandhi's focus on empowering young people, promoting gender equality, and building a more inclusive and equitable society reflects his vision for a more dynamic, diverse, and prosperous India.

# 6. Rahul Gandhi's views on foreign policy and India's role in the global community

Rahul Gandhi's views on foreign policy and India's role in the global community are based on promoting India's interests while also promoting peace and stability in the world. He believes that India has a critical role to play in the global community and that it is essential to build strong relationships with other countries based on mutual respect and cooperation.

One of the key elements of Rahul Gandhi's approach to foreign policy is his focus on multilateralism. He believes that India should work closely with other countries and international organizations to address global challenges, such as climate change, terrorism, and economic inequality. Rahul Gandhi has emphasized the importance of India playing a leadership role in these efforts and has called for increased investment in multilateral institutions, such as the United Nations.

Rahul Gandhi's approach to foreign policy also emphasizes the importance of promoting human rights and democracy. He has been vocal in his support for human rights and has called for greater protection of civil liberties and freedom of speech in India and in other countries. Rahul Gandhi has also emphasized the importance of promoting democratic values and institutions around the world, and has called for greater cooperation between democratic countries to promote global stability.

Another important element of Rahul Gandhi's approach to foreign policy is his focus on economic diplomacy. He believes that India should prioritize economic growth and development in its relations with other countries, and has called for increased investment in trade and investment. Rahul Gandhi also emphasizes the importance of promoting Indian businesses and entrepreneurs in the global market, and has called for policies and programs that support these efforts.

Overall, Rahul Gandhi's views on foreign policy and India's role in the global community reflect his commitment to promoting India's interests while also promoting peace, stability, and democracy around the world. His emphasis on multilateralism, human rights, and economic diplomacy reflects his vision for a more engaged, responsible, and prosperous India in the global arena.

# 7. Rahul Gandhi's vision for a more transparent and accountable government in India

Rahul Gandhi's vision for a more transparent and accountable government in India is based on the belief that good governance is essential for promoting democracy, development, and social justice. He believes that the government must be accountable to the people and that transparency is essential for building trust and confidence in government institutions.

One of the key elements of Rahul Gandhi's approach to transparency and accountability is his focus on anti-corruption measures. He has been vocal in his support for greater transparency in government procurement processes and has called for the implementation of anti-corruption laws that promote accountability and punish corrupt officials. Rahul Gandhi has also emphasized the importance of whistleblowers in exposing corruption and has called for greater protection for those who speak out against corruption.

Rahul Gandhi's approach to transparency and accountability also emphasizes the importance of strengthening democratic institutions. He believes that it is essential to promote greater citizen participation in decision-making processes and has called for policies and programs that promote greater transparency in political party funding, electoral processes, and public policymaking.

Another important element of Rahul Gandhi's approach to transparency and accountability is his focus on technology. He believes that technology can play a critical role in promoting transparency and accountability in government institutions, and has called for greater use of technology to provide citizens with access to information and government services. Rahul Gandhi has also emphasized the importance of data privacy and cybersecurity, and has called for policies and programs that protect citizens' data and digital rights.

Overall, Rahul Gandhi's vision for a more transparent and accountable government in India reflects his commitment to promoting democracy, development, and social justice. His emphasis on anti-corruption measures, strengthening democratic institutions, and technology reflects his vision for a more open, responsive, and responsible government in India.

# 8. The role of technology in promoting good governance in Rahul Gandhi's approach

The role of technology is a key element of Rahul Gandhi's approach to promoting good governance in India. He believes that technology can play a critical role in promoting transparency, accountability, and citizen participation in government institutions.

One of the key ways in which Rahul Gandhi believes technology can promote good governance is through the use of e-governance platforms. He has called for the development of user-friendly, accessible, and secure e-governance platforms that can provide citizens with access to government services and information. Rahul Gandhi believes that e-governance platforms can help to reduce bureaucracy, corruption, and red tape in government processes, and can promote greater efficiency and effectiveness in government delivery systems.

Rahul Gandhi also believes that technology can promote citizen participation in government decision-making processes. He has called for the development of online forums, discussion boards, and other digital platforms that can enable citizens to engage with government officials and policymakers, and provide feedback on government policies and programs. Rahul Gandhi believes that such platforms can help to promote greater transparency, accountability, and responsiveness in government decision-making.

Another important element of Rahul Gandhi's approach to technology and good governance is his focus on digital literacy and skills development. He believes that it is essential to provide citizens with the skills and knowledge they need to effectively use digital platforms and engage with government institutions. Rahul Gandhi has called for policies and programs that promote digital literacy and skills development, especially in rural and marginalized communities.

Overall, the role of technology is a critical element of Rahul Gandhi's approach to promoting good governance in India. He believes that technology can help to promote transparency, accountability, and citizen participation, and can lead to greater efficiency, effectiveness, and responsiveness in government institutions. Rahul Gandhi's focus on e-governance, citizen participation, and digital literacy reflects his vision for a more open, democratic, and responsive government in India.

# 9. Rahul Gandhi's emphasis on environmental sustainability and climate action

Rahul Gandhi's emphasis on environmental sustainability and climate action is based on the recognition that climate change is one of the most pressing global challenges of our time. He believes that India has a critical role to play in addressing climate change and promoting sustainable development.

One of the key elements of Rahul Gandhi's approach to environmental sustainability is his focus on renewable energy. He has called for greater investment in solar, wind, and other forms of renewable energy, as well as policies and programs that promote energy efficiency and conservation. Rahul Gandhi believes that a shift towards renewable energy is essential for reducing greenhouse gas emissions and promoting sustainable development.

Rahul Gandhi's approach to environmental sustainability also emphasizes the importance of environmental protection and conservation. He has called for policies and programs that protect forests, wetlands, and other critical ecosystems, and that promote biodiversity conservation. Rahul Gandhi believes that protecting the environment is essential for promoting sustainable development and ensuring the well-being of future generations.

Another important element of Rahul Gandhi's approach to environmental sustainability is his focus on sustainable agriculture and food systems. He believes that it is essential to promote sustainable agricultural practices that reduce the environmental impact of farming and promote food security. Rahul Gandhi has called for policies and programs that promote organic farming, agroforestry, and sustainable livestock management, and that support small farmers and rural communities.

Overall, Rahul Gandhi's emphasis on environmental sustainability and climate action reflects his commitment to promoting sustainable development and ensuring that India plays a leadership role in addressing global environmental challenges. His focus on renewable energy, environmental protection, and sustainable agriculture reflects his vision for a more sustainable, equitable, and prosperous India.

# 10. The importance of promoting democracy and human rights in Rahul Gandhi's ideology

The promotion of democracy and human rights is a core element of Rahul Gandhi's ideology. He believes that democracy and human rights are fundamental to building a just, equitable, and inclusive society, and that it is the responsibility of the government to protect and promote these values.

One of the key elements of Rahul Gandhi's approach to democracy is his focus on promoting citizen participation and engagement in political processes. He has called for policies and programs that promote greater citizen participation in decision-making processes, such as participatory budgeting and community-based planning. Rahul Gandhi believes that citizen participation is essential for promoting transparency, accountability, and responsiveness in government institutions.

Rahul Gandhi's approach to human rights also emphasizes the importance of protecting civil liberties and promoting human dignity. He has been vocal in his support for freedom of speech, freedom of the press, and other civil liberties, and has called for greater protection of these rights in India and around the world. Rahul Gandhi believes that protecting human rights is essential for promoting democracy, peace, and social justice.

Another important element of Rahul Gandhi's approach to democracy and human rights is his focus on promoting gender equality and women's empowerment. He believes that women's rights are fundamental human rights, and has called for policies and programs that promote women's empowerment and address gender-based discrimination and violence. Rahul Gandhi has emphasized the importance of greater representation of women in political and economic decision-making, and has advocated for policies that promote equal pay and access to education and healthcare for women.

Overall, the promotion of democracy and human rights is central to Rahul Gandhi's ideology. He believes that democracy and human rights are essential for building a just, equitable, and inclusive society, and that it is the responsibility of the government to protect and promote these values. Rahul Gandhi's emphasis on citizen participation, human dignity, and gender equality reflects his vision for a more democratic, peaceful, and socially just India.

# 11. The legacy of the Gandhi-Nehru family and its influence on Rahul Gandhi's ideology and vision for India.

The legacy of the Gandhi-Nehru family has had a profound influence on Rahul Gandhi's ideology and vision for India. Rahul Gandhi is the scion of one of India's most prominent political families, and comes from a long line of politicians and social reformers who played a critical role in shaping modern India.

The Gandhi-Nehru family's legacy is rooted in their commitment to democracy, social justice, and secularism. Rahul Gandhi's great-grandfather, Jawaharlal Nehru, was India's first prime minister and played a key role in shaping India's secular, democratic, and socialist identity. Nehru's emphasis on science, education, and modernization helped to lay the foundation for India's post-independence development.

Rahul Gandhi's grandmother, Indira Gandhi, was also an influential political figure who served as India's prime minister for three terms. Indira Gandhi's emphasis on economic development and social justice helped to transform India's economy and expand access to education, healthcare, and other basic services.

Rajiv Gandhi, Rahul Gandhi's father, continued the family legacy of promoting democratic values and social development. Rajiv Gandhi's commitment to modernization and technology helped to usher in a new era of economic growth and development in India.

Rahul Gandhi's vision for India reflects his family's legacy of promoting democracy, social justice, and secularism. He has emphasized the importance of citizen participation in decision-making processes, and has called for policies and programs that promote greater transparency, accountability, and responsiveness in government institutions. Rahul Gandhi's focus on environmental sustainability, renewable energy, and sustainable agriculture reflects his family's commitment to social and economic development that benefits all citizens.

Overall, the Gandhi-Nehru family's legacy has had a significant influence on Rahul Gandhi's ideology and vision for India. Rahul Gandhi's emphasis on democracy, social justice, and environmental sustainability reflects a continuation of the family's commitment to building a just, equitable, and inclusive society in India.

# 12. Key policy positions and initiatives

Rahul Gandhi has taken a number of key policy positions and initiatives in his political career. Some of the most notable include:

1. Promoting social justice: Rahul Gandhi has been a vocal advocate for social justice and has worked to empower marginalized communities, including farmers, laborers, and women. He has supported policies such as the National Rural Employment Guarantee Act (NREGA) to reduce poverty and increase social mobility.

2. Environmental protection: Rahul Gandhi has been a vocal proponent of environmental protection and has spoken out against climate change. He has advocated for policies that promote sustainable development and reduce reliance on fossil fuels.

3. Empowering youth: Rahul Gandhi has worked to increase youth participation in Indian politics through initiatives such as the Indian Youth Congress and the National Students Union of India. He has also focused on promoting the education and employment of young people.

4. Strengthening democratic institutions: Rahul Gandhi has been a vocal critic of attempts to undermine democratic institutions in India, and has advocated for the protection of free speech and press freedom. He has also sought to increase transparency and accountability in government.

5. Supporting entrepreneurship: Rahul Gandhi has supported policies that promote entrepreneurship, particularly among women and marginalized communities. He has advocated for increased access to credit and other resources, as well as for the development of skills and training programs.

Overall, Rahul Gandhi's policy positions and initiatives reflect a commitment to social justice, environmental protection, and democratic values. While his ideas and policy positions have faced criticism and controversy at times, his dedication to these values has earned him a significant following in India and around the world.

# 13. Critiques and challenges to his vision

R ahul Gandhi's vision for India has faced a number of critiques and challenges over the years. Some of the most common critiques include:

1.  Lack of clarity: Rahul Gandhi's policy positions and vision for India have been criticized for lacking clarity and specificity. Some have argued that his ideas are too broad and lack concrete details on how they will be implemented.
2.  Inexperience: Rahul Gandhi has faced criticism for his perceived lack of experience and hesitancy in making bold policy decisions. Some have argued that he has yet to prove himself as a capable leader.
3.  Poor electoral performance: The Congress party has suffered a number of electoral defeats under Rahul Gandhi's leadership, including a crushing defeat in the 2014 Lok Sabha elections. This has led some to question his ability to lead the party effectively.
4.  Perception of entitlement: Rahul Gandhi has been criticized for his perceived sense of entitlement, as he comes from a prominent political family. This has led some to question his ability to connect with ordinary citizens and understand their needs and concerns.

Despite these critiques and challenges, Rahul Gandhi's vision for India continues to resonate with many people, particularly those who are marginalized or have been left behind by economic growth. His commitment to social justice, environmental protection, and democratic values has earned him a significant following in India and around the world, and his ideas and policy positions continue to shape the political discourse in India.

One of the most common critiques of Rahul Gandhi's political vision for India is that it lacks clarity and specificity. While he has articulated a broad commitment to social justice, economic equality, and environmental protection, some have argued that his ideas are too vague and lack concrete details on how they will be implemented.

Critics have pointed out that Rahul Gandhi's policy positions often lack the level of detail necessary to convince voters and stakeholders of their feasibility and effectiveness. This has led to a perception that his vision for India is more aspirational than practical, and that it is not grounded in a clear understanding of the challenges facing the country.

Some have also argued that Rahul Gandhi's perceived lack of clarity has contributed to a lack of confidence in his leadership abilities. While he has shown a willingness to take on difficult issues, such as the rights of marginalized communities and environmental protection, critics argue that he has yet to provide a clear roadmap for how these issues will be addressed.

Despite these critiques, Rahul Gandhi's vision for India has resonated with many people, particularly those who believe that the current political and economic system is leaving them behind. While he may face challenges in articulating a clear and actionable political vision, his commitment to social justice, economic equality, and environmental protection continues to inspire many in India and around the world.

Another common critique of Rahul Gandhi's political career is his perceived lack of experience and hesitancy in making bold policy decisions. Some argue that he has yet to prove himself as a capable leader and that his inexperience could hinder his ability to lead effectively.

While Rahul Gandhi has been active in politics for many years, some argue that his upbringing in a political family has shielded him from the kind of challenges faced by ordinary citizens. This has led to a perception that he may lack the empathy and understanding necessary to connect with voters and to make informed policy decisions.

Critics have also pointed out that Rahul Gandhi has not held a significant executive role in government, which has limited his exposure to the complexities of policymaking and governance. While he has served as a Member of Parliament and as Vice President of the Indian National Congress, some argue that this is not enough to prepare him for the demands of the Prime Minister's office.

Despite these critiques, supporters of Rahul Gandhi point to his commitment to social justice, economic equality, and environmental protection as evidence of his leadership potential. While he may lack experience in some areas, they argue that his dedication to these issues and his willingness to take on difficult challenges make him a valuable voice in Indian politics.

Rahul Gandhi has faced criticism for the poor electoral performance of the Congress party under his leadership. The party suffered a crushing defeat in the 2014 Lok Sabha elections, winning just 44 seats out of 543. This was seen as a major setback for the party, which had previously been a dominant force in Indian politics.

Critics have argued that Rahul Gandhi's leadership style and policy positions have failed to resonate with voters, particularly younger voters who are looking for more dynamic and innovative political leadership. Some have also criticized the Congress party's perceived lack of organizational strength and ground-level engagement, which they argue has contributed to its poor electoral performance.

Rahul Gandhi's political career has been dogged by accusations of entitlement, as he comes from a prominent political family. His family has been a dominant force in Indian politics for several generations, which has led to a perception that he is more interested in preserving his family's political legacy than in serving the needs of ordinary citizens.

Critics argue that Rahul Gandhi's perceived sense of entitlement has hindered his ability to connect with voters from diverse backgrounds and to understand their needs and concerns. Some have also criticized his apparent reluctance to take on more challenging policy positions or to engage in more direct political confrontation, which they argue reflects a lack of commitment to the challenges facing the country.

Despite these critiques, Rahul Gandhi's commitment to social justice, economic equality, and environmental protection continues to inspire many in India and around the world. While he may have faced challenges in articulating a clear and actionable political vision, his dedication to these values and his willingness to take on difficult issues has earned him a significant following among those who believe in the power of government to promote the common good.

# V. Rahul Gandhi and the Congress Party

Rahul Gandhi has been a prominent figure in the Congress Party for many years, and has played an active role in shaping its political direction and policy positions. He was appointed Vice President of the party in 2013, and later became its President in 2017.

Under Rahul Gandhi's leadership, the Congress Party has sought to promote a vision of India that is committed to social justice, economic equality, and environmental protection. He has been a vocal advocate for the rights of marginalized communities, including farmers, laborers, and women, and has worked to empower these communities by providing them with access to education, healthcare, and other resources.

Despite these efforts, the Congress Party has faced significant challenges in recent years, including a series of electoral defeats in state and national elections. This has led to criticism of Rahul Gandhi's leadership and policy positions, with some arguing that he has failed to connect with voters and to provide a clear and compelling political vision for the party and for India as a whole.

Despite these challenges, Rahul Gandhi remains committed to the Congress Party and to his vision for India. He has sought to build a stronger and more inclusive party, and has continued to speak out on issues that he believes are important, such as climate change, social justice, and democratic values. While the future of the Congress Party remains uncertain, Rahul Gandhi's leadership and commitment to these values continue to inspire many in India and around the world.

# 1. Rahul Gandhi's role within the Congress party

Rahul Gandhi has played a prominent role in the Congress Party over the course of his political career. He was appointed Vice President of the party in 2013, and later became its President in 2017. During this time, he has sought to promote a vision of India that is committed to social justice, economic equality, and environmental protection.

As Vice President, Rahul Gandhi played an active role in shaping the party's policies and political direction. He was a vocal advocate for the rights of marginalized communities, including farmers, laborers, and women, and worked to empower these communities by providing them with access to education, healthcare, and other resources.

As President of the Congress Party, Rahul Gandhi continued to build on this vision, seeking to create a stronger and more inclusive party that could better represent the interests of all Indians. He has spoken out on issues such as climate change, social justice, and democratic values, and has worked to strengthen the party's organizational structure and ground-level engagement.

Despite these efforts, the Congress Party has faced significant challenges in recent years, including a series of electoral defeats in state and national elections. This has led to criticism of Rahul Gandhi's leadership and policy positions, with some arguing that he has failed to connect with voters and to provide a clear and compelling political vision for the party and for India as a whole.

Despite these challenges, Rahul Gandhi's role within the Congress Party remains a significant one. His advocacy for marginalized communities and commitment to social justice, economic equality, and environmental protection continue to inspire many in India and around the world. While the future of the Congress Party remains uncertain, Rahul Gandhi's leadership and dedication to these values will continue to shape the party's direction and political discourse in India.

# 2. Rahul Gandhi was elected president of the Indian National Congress party in December 2017, succeeding his mother Sonia Gandhi.

Rahul Gandhi succeeded his mother Sonia Gandhi as the president of the Indian National Congress party in December 2017. Sonia Gandhi had been the party's president for nearly two decades before stepping down due to health reasons. Rahul Gandhi's tenure as the party president, however, was short-lived as he resigned in 2019 following the party's poor performance in the general elections.

# 3. The Indian National Congress party is one of the two major political parties in India, along with the Bharatiya Janata Party (BJP). The party was founded in 1885 and played a key role in India's struggle for independence against British rule.

The Indian National Congress party is one of the two major political parties in India, along with the Bharatiya Janata Party (BJP). The party was founded in 1885 by Allan Octavian Hume, Dadabhai Naoroji, and Dinshaw Wacha, with the aim of seeking greater representation for Indians in the British colonial government. Over time, the party became a key player in India's struggle for independence against British rule, with leaders like Mahatma Gandhi and Jawaharlal Nehru playing a prominent role in the movement. Today, the Congress party remains an important political force in India, with a presence in various state governments and at the national level.

# 4. The Congress party has governed India for a total of 54 years since independence in 1947, including under the leadership of Jawaharlal Nehru, Indira Gandhi, and Rajiv Gandhi.

The Congress party has been in power for a total of 54 years since India gained independence from British rule in 1947. Some of the most prominent Congress leaders who have served as Prime Minister of India include Jawaharlal Nehru, Indira Gandhi, and Rajiv Gandhi. Nehru, who was India's first Prime Minister, led the country from 1947 until his death in 1964. His daughter, Indira Gandhi, served as Prime Minister from 1966 to 1977 and again from 1980 until her assassination in 1984. Rajiv Gandhi, who was Indira Gandhi's son and Rahul Gandhi's father, served as Prime Minister from 1984 until 1989.

# 5. The party has been associated with the promotion of secularism, social democracy, and economic liberalization in India.

The Congress party has been associated with the promotion of secularism, social democracy, and economic liberalization in India. The party has advocated for a secular, inclusive society where people of all religions and communities have equal rights and opportunities. It has also championed social welfare policies aimed at reducing poverty and improving access to education and healthcare. In terms of economic policy, the Congress party has supported liberalization measures aimed at promoting growth and development, such as deregulation, privatization, and foreign investment. However, the party has also faced criticism from some quarters for its role in the economic liberalization process, particularly for allegedly neglecting the needs of marginalized communities and exacerbating income inequality.

# 6. The Congress party has faced criticism in recent years for alleged corruption and a decline in electoral support, particularly in the 2014 and 2019 general elections. However, it continues to be a major political force in India.

The Congress party has faced criticism in recent years for alleged corruption and a decline in electoral support, particularly in the 2014 and 2019 general elections. The party's poor performance in these elections has led to questions about its ability to remain a major political force in India. However, the Congress party remains an important political entity in India, with a presence in various state governments and at the national level. It continues to advocate for its vision of a secular, inclusive and economically developed India, and remains a key player in Indian politics.

# 7. Interactions with other party members and leaders

As a prominent figure within the Congress Party, Rahul Gandhi has had numerous interactions with other party members and leaders over the course of his political career. He has sought to build consensus and promote a more inclusive and vibrant political culture within the party, while also working to advance his own policy priorities.

Rahul Gandhi has been known to engage in direct and informal conversations with party members and leaders at all levels, from grassroots workers to senior officials. He has sought to build personal relationships with these individuals, and has often worked to identify and cultivate new talent within the party.

At the same time, Rahul Gandhi has faced criticism from some quarters for his perceived reluctance to engage in more direct political confrontation with other party leaders. Some have argued that this has contributed to a lack of clarity and direction within the party, and has hindered its ability to effectively oppose the policies of the ruling government.

Despite these challenges, Rahul Gandhi's interactions with other party members and leaders continue to shape the Congress Party's political direction and discourse. His commitment to social justice, economic equality, and environmental protection has earned him a significant following within the party, and he remains a prominent voice in Indian politics. While the future of the Congress Party remains uncertain, Rahul Gandhi's leadership and dedication to these values will continue to play an important role in shaping the party's direction and political fortunes.

# 8. Controversies and challenges within the Congress party

The Congress Party has faced numerous controversies and challenges in recent years, ranging from electoral defeats to internal divisions. These challenges have posed significant difficulties for the party and its leadership, including Rahul Gandhi.

One of the most significant challenges facing the Congress Party has been its inability to effectively counter the policies of the ruling government. Despite Rahul Gandhi's efforts to build a stronger and more inclusive party, the party has struggled to mobilize its base and to effectively articulate a clear and compelling political vision for the country.

In addition to these challenges, the Congress Party has also faced criticism for its internal divisions and factionalism. Some have argued that these divisions have hindered the party's ability to effectively challenge the ruling government and to promote a united and inclusive political culture.

Another controversial issue within the Congress Party has been the role of dynastic politics in the party's leadership structure. Rahul Gandhi comes from a prominent political family, and some have argued that this has led to a perception of entitlement among party leaders and a lack of true democratic engagement within the party.

Despite these challenges and controversies, the Congress Party remains a significant force in Indian politics, and Rahul Gandhi's leadership continues to shape the party's direction and political discourse. While the future of the party remains uncertain, Rahul Gandhi's commitment to social justice, economic equality, and environmental protection will continue to inspire many in India and around the world.

# 9. Understand the political philosophy and vision of Rahul Gandhi

Rahul Gandhi's political philosophy centres around social justice, economic equality, and environmental protection. He believes that India must work towards a more inclusive society where all individuals have access to basic resources like education, healthcare, and livelihood opportunities, regardless of their social or economic status.

Rahul Gandhi is committed to promoting the rights of marginalized communities, including women, Dalits, Adivasis, and religious minorities. He has spoken out against discrimination and violence directed towards these groups, and has advocated for policies that empower them and provide them greater access to resources and opportunities.

In terms of economic policy, Rahul Gandhi believes that India must focus on reducing inequality and ensuring that the benefits of economic growth are shared more equitably across society. He advocates for policies that provide greater support for small and medium-sized businesses, and for increased investment in education, healthcare, and infrastructure.

Finally, Rahul Gandhi is a vocal advocate for environmental protection and sustainability. He believes that India must transition to a clean energy economy and reduce its carbon emissions to combat climate change. He has spoken out against environmental degradation, deforestation, and pollution, and has called for greater investment in renewable energy and sustainable development.

Overall, Rahul Gandhi's political philosophy is centered on promoting a more just and equitable society that prioritizes the needs and rights of marginalized communities and protects the environment for future generations.

# VI. Rahul Gandhi and Indian Politics

Rahul Gandhi has been a prominent figure in Indian politics for many years, and has played an active role in shaping the direction of the country. As a leader within the Congress Party, Rahul Gandhi has sought to promote a vision of India that is committed to social justice, economic equality, and environmental protection.

He has been a vocal advocate for the rights of marginalized communities, including farmers, laborers, and women, and has worked to empower these communities by providing them with access to education, healthcare, and other resources.

Rahul Gandhi has also been a strong proponent of democratic values and institutions, and has spoken out against attempts to undermine these values through the use of authoritarian tactics or the suppression of dissent. He has been a vocal critic of the ruling government's policies on a range of issues, including economic inequality, environmental degradation, and the erosion of civil liberties.

Despite criticism of his leadership and policy positions, Rahul Gandhi remains a significant figure in Indian politics, with a significant following among those who believe in the power of government to promote the common good. While the future of the Congress Party remains uncertain, Rahul Gandhi's dedication to social justice, economic equality, and environmental protection will continue to shape the direction of Indian politics and inspire those who seek to build a more just and equitable society.

# 1. The impact of Rahul Gandhi on Indian politics

Rahul Gandhi has had a significant impact on Indian politics over the course of his career. As a leader within the Congress Party, he has sought to promote a vision of India that is committed to social justice, economic equality, and environmental protection.

His advocacy for the rights of marginalized communities and his commitment to democratic values and institutions have inspired many in India and around the world. He has been a vocal critic of the ruling government's policies on a range of issues, including economic inequality, environmental degradation, and the erosion of civil liberties.

Despite some criticism of his leadership and policy positions, Rahul Gandhi's dedication to these values has earned him a significant following among those who believe in the power of government to promote the common good. His leadership and activism have helped to shape the political discourse in India and to advance a more inclusive and progressive agenda for the country.

Rahul Gandhi's impact on Indian politics is likely to be felt for many years to come, as his vision of a more just and equitable society continues to inspire those who seek to build a better future for India and its people. While the future of the Congress Party remains uncertain, Rahul Gandhi's leadership and dedication to these values will continue to shape the direction of Indian politics and inspire those who seek to create a more just and equitable society.

1. Promoting Social Justice: Rahul Gandhi has been a vocal advocate for the rights of marginalized communities in India, including women, Dalits, Adivasis, and religious minorities. He has championed policies to empower these communities, such as quotas for women in elected bodies and greater access to education and healthcare.

2. Advocating for Economic Equality: Rahul Gandhi has promoted policies to reduce economic inequality in India, such as increased

investment in education and healthcare, greater support for small and medium-sized businesses, and job creation in rural areas. His advocacy for greater economic equality has helped to shift the political discourse in India towards issues of social welfare and redistribution.

3. Opposing Authoritarianism: Rahul Gandhi has been a vocal critic of the ruling government's policies, particularly on issues such as civil liberties, freedom of speech, and minority rights. He has spoken out against the growing trend of authoritarianism in India and has called for the protection of democratic institutions and values.

4. Promoting Environmental Protection: Rahul Gandhi has been a strong advocate for environmental protection and sustainability. He has called for India to transition to a clean energy economy, reduce its carbon emissions, and protect its natural resources from degradation and exploitation.

5. Rebuilding the Congress Party: Rahul Gandhi has played a key role in rebuilding the Congress Party and in promoting a more united and inclusive political culture within the party. Despite facing challenges such as electoral defeats and internal divisions, he has remained committed to promoting a more progressive and inclusive political agenda.

Overall, Rahul Gandhi's impact on Indian politics has been significant, particularly in his advocacy for social justice, economic equality, and democratic values. His leadership and vision have helped to shape the political discourse in India and to promote a more inclusive and progressive agenda for the country.

Promoting Social Justice:

Promoting social justice is one of Rahul Gandhi's key priorities in Indian politics. He has consistently advocated for policies and initiatives that empower marginalized communities and promote greater inclusion and equity.

One of Rahul Gandhi's most notable contributions to promoting social justice in India has been his advocacy for the rights of women. He has called for greater representation of women in politics and has championed policies to enhance women's access to education and healthcare. Rahul Gandhi has also advocated for greater legal protections for women, including stronger laws against sexual harassment and domestic violence.

In addition to his work on women's rights, Rahul Gandhi has also been a vocal advocate for the rights of Dalits, Adivasis, and religious minorities. He has spoken out against discrimination and violence directed towards these groups, and has called for policies to empower them and provide greater access to resources and opportunities.

Rahul Gandhi has also been a strong advocate for greater access to education and healthcare for all Indians. He has called for increased investment in these sectors, particularly in rural areas where access to these resources is often limited. Rahul Gandhi has also advocated for policies to enhance the quality of education and healthcare services, and to increase access to them for marginalized communities.

Overall, Rahul Gandhi's advocacy for social justice has helped to promote greater inclusion and equity in Indian society. His leadership and vision have inspired many in India and around the world to work towards a more just and equitable future.

Advocating for Economic Equality:

Advocating for economic equality is another key priority for Rahul Gandhi in Indian politics. He has consistently advocated for policies and initiatives that reduce economic inequality and promote greater access to resources and opportunities.

One of Rahul Gandhi's most notable contributions to promoting economic equality in India has been his advocacy for greater support for small and medium-sized businesses. He has called for policies that provide greater access to credit and finance for these businesses, and has advocated for measures to reduce red tape and bureaucratic hurdles that can hinder their growth.

In addition to his work on promoting small and medium-sized businesses, Rahul Gandhi has also been a strong advocate for job creation in rural areas. He has called for policies to enhance agricultural productivity and to promote rural entrepreneurship, and has advocated for greater investment in infrastructure and connectivity in rural areas.

Rahul Gandhi has also been a vocal critic of economic policies that exacerbate economic inequality, such as the privatization of public resources and the concentration of wealth in the hands of a few powerful individuals.

He has called for policies that reduce economic inequality, such as progressive taxation and increased investment in social welfare programs.

Overall, Rahul Gandhi's advocacy for economic equality has helped to shift the political discourse in India towards issues of social welfare and redistribution. His leadership and vision have inspired many in India and around the world to work towards a more inclusive and equitable economy that benefits all members of society.

## OPPOSING AUTHORITARIANISM:

Opposing authoritarianism is another key concern for Rahul Gandhi in Indian politics. He has been a vocal critic of the ruling government's policies, particularly on issues related to civil liberties, freedom of expression, and minority rights. Rahul Gandhi has called for the protection of democratic institutions and values, and has been a strong advocate for greater transparency and accountability in government.

One of Rahul Gandhi's most notable contributions to opposing authoritarianism in India has been his criticism of the government's policies on freedom of expression. He has spoken out against the government's attempts to suppress dissent and to restrict access to information, and has called for greater protection of the rights of journalists and other members of the media.

Rahul Gandhi has also been a vocal advocate for minority rights in India. He has spoken out against discrimination and violence directed towards religious minorities, and has called for policies that promote greater inclusion and equity for all members of society. Rahul Gandhi has been a vocal critic of the government's policies on citizenship and has opposed the controversial Citizenship Amendment Act (CAA) which he claims is discriminatory against Muslims.

Rahul Gandhi has also been a strong advocate for the protection of democratic institutions in India. He has called for greater transparency and accountability in government, and has criticized the government's attempts to restrict the functioning of institutions such as the judiciary and the electoral commission.

Overall, Rahul Gandhi's opposition to authoritarianism has been a significant contribution to Indian politics. His leadership and advocacy have helped to promote greater transparency, accountability, and protection of democratic institutions and values, and have inspired many in India and around the world to work towards a more democratic and just society.

# 2. Rahul Gandhi is a member of the Indian National Congress party and has been involved in Indian politics for over a decade. He was elected to the Lok Sabha, the lower house of the Indian Parliament, for the first time in 2004.

Rahul Gandhi has been involved in Indian politics for over a decade and is a member of the Indian National Congress party. He was first elected to the Lok Sabha, the lower house of the Indian Parliament, in 2004, representing the Amethi constituency in Uttar Pradesh state. Since then, he has been re-elected from the same constituency in the 2009 and 2014 general elections. However, in the 2019 general elections, Rahul Gandhi lost his seat in Amethi to his Bharatiya Janata Party (BJP) rival. Despite this setback, Rahul Gandhi continues to be an important figure in Indian politics, and is widely seen as a potential future Prime Minister of India.

# 3. Rahul Gandhi has been a vocal critic of the policies of the ruling Bharatiya Janata Party (BJP), particularly on issues such as demonetization and the implementation of the Goods and Services Tax (GST).

Rahul Gandhi has been a vocal critic of the policies of the ruling Bharatiya Janata Party (BJP), particularly on issues such as demonetization and the implementation of the Goods and Services Tax (GST). In 2016, the BJP government announced a sudden demonetization of high-value currency notes, which was aimed at curbing corruption and black money. However, the move was widely criticized by opposition parties, including the Congress, for its impact on the economy and the common people. Similarly, the GST, which was introduced in 2017, was also criticized by the Congress for its impact on small and medium-sized businesses. Rahul Gandhi has been a leading voice in the opposition to these policies, and has consistently called for more inclusive and equitable economic policies that benefit all sections of Indian society.

# 4. Rahul Gandhi has also been involved in several social and developmental initiatives, such as the Rajiv Gandhi Foundation and the National Students Union of India.

Rahul Gandhi has been involved in several social and developmental initiatives during his tenure in Indian politics. He has worked with the Rajiv Gandhi Foundation, a non-profit organization that promotes sustainable development in India, and has also been associated with the National Students Union of India (NSUI), the student wing of the Congress party. As part of his work with these organizations, Rahul Gandhi has advocated for policies that promote education, healthcare, and social welfare, and has worked to empower marginalized communities and promote their participation in the political process. He has also been involved in initiatives aimed at promoting entrepreneurship and economic growth, particularly in rural areas. Through his work in these areas, Rahul Gandhi has sought to build a more inclusive and equitable India that benefits all its citizens.

# 5. Rahul Gandhi is known for his efforts to connect with young people and bring them into the political process. He has been involved in several initiatives aimed at engaging young people and promoting their participation in politics.

Rahul Gandhi is known for his efforts to connect with young people and encourage them to participate in the political process. He has been involved in several initiatives aimed at engaging young people, such as the Indian Youth Congress and the National Students Union of India. Through these organizations, Rahul Gandhi has sought to create opportunities for young people to participate in politics and make their voices heard. He has also been active on social media platforms such as Twitter and Instagram, where he has a large following among young people. Rahul Gandhi's efforts to engage with young people reflect his belief in the importance of building a more inclusive and participatory democracy in India, where all citizens have a say in shaping the country's future.

# 6. Despite the criticism, Rahul Gandhi remains a prominent figure in Indian politics and is likely to continue to play an influential role in the future.

Rahul Gandhi has been the subject of both praise and criticism from various quarters. While some view him as a charismatic leader with a strong vision for India's future, others criticize him for his lack of experience and perceived inability to connect with voters. Despite the criticism, Rahul Gandhi remains a prominent figure in Indian politics and is likely to continue to play an influential role in the future. He has been a vocal advocate for the rights of farmers, workers, and marginalized communities, and has sought to build a more inclusive India that benefits all its citizens. With his experience in Indian politics and his strong commitment to social and economic justice, Rahul Gandhi is expected to remain a key player in Indian politics for years to come.

# 7. The challenges and opportunities for his political future

Rahul Gandhi faces significant challenges and opportunities as he considers his political future. While he remains a prominent figure in Indian politics and has a significant following among those who share his commitment to social justice, economic equality, and environmental protection, he faces numerous obstacles in his efforts to promote a more inclusive and progressive political agenda.

One of the biggest challenges facing Rahul Gandhi is the ongoing crisis within the Congress Party. The party has faced a series of electoral defeats in recent years, and has struggled to effectively challenge the policies of the ruling government. Rahul Gandhi will need to find ways to revitalize the party and to build a more united and inclusive political culture if he hopes to make further gains in the coming years.

Another challenge for Rahul Gandhi is the perception of entitlement and dynastic politics that has been associated with his family's political legacy. Some have argued that this perception has hindered his ability to connect with voters and to effectively articulate a clear and compelling political vision for the country.

Despite these challenges, Rahul Gandhi also has significant opportunities for the future. He remains a prominent voice in Indian politics and has a significant following among those who share his commitment to social justice, economic equality, and environmental protection. He has the potential to build a more united and inclusive Congress Party, and to lead a more effective opposition to the policies of the ruling government.

Ultimately, the challenges and opportunities for Rahul Gandhi's political future will depend on his ability to effectively mobilize support, to build consensus within the Congress Party, and to articulate a clear and compelling political vision for the country. While the road ahead will not be easy, Rahul

Gandhi's dedication to these values and his commitment to the common good provide a powerful foundation for his future political endeavors.

Promoting Environmental Protection:

Promoting environmental protection is another key priority for Rahul Gandhi in Indian politics. He has been a strong advocate for sustainability and has called for policies that promote a transition to a clean energy economy and reduce India's carbon emissions.

One of Rahul Gandhi's most notable contributions to promoting environmental protection in India has been his advocacy for renewable energy. He has called for greater investment in solar, wind, and other forms of renewable energy, and has advocated for policies that promote energy efficiency and conservation. Rahul Gandhi has also been a vocal critic of the government's policies on coal and other fossil fuels, and has called for a shift away from these resources towards cleaner sources of energy.

Rahul Gandhi has also been a strong advocate for protecting India's natural resources from degradation and exploitation. He has spoken out against deforestation, pollution, and other forms of environmental degradation, and has called for policies that promote sustainable development and protect the rights of local communities.

In addition to his work on promoting renewable energy and protecting natural resources, Rahul Gandhi has also advocated for policies that promote sustainable agriculture and reduce food waste. He has called for greater investment in organic farming, and has advocated for policies that promote greater access to nutritious food for all Indians.

Overall, Rahul Gandhi's advocacy for environmental protection has helped to promote greater sustainability and resilience in Indian society. His leadership and vision have inspired many in India and around the world to work towards a more sustainable future that protects the environment and promotes social and economic equity.

Rebuilding the Congress Party:

Rebuilding the Congress Party is another key priority for Rahul Gandhi in Indian politics. He has played a prominent role in the party's leadership, and has worked to promote a more united and inclusive political culture within the party.

One of Rahul Gandhi's most notable contributions to rebuilding the Congress Party has been his focus on promoting greater inclusion of young people and women in the party's leadership. He has called for greater representation of these groups in the party's decision-making bodies, and has championed policies that promote their empowerment and access to resources and opportunities.

Rahul Gandhi has also been a vocal advocate for greater internal democracy within the Congress Party. He has called for greater transparency and accountability in the party's functioning, and has advocated for policies that promote greater engagement with the party's grassroots supporters.

In addition to his work on promoting greater inclusion and internal democracy in the Congress Party, Rahul Gandhi has also focused on promoting a more progressive political agenda. He has advocated for policies that promote social welfare and redistribution, and has called for greater investment in education, healthcare, and infrastructure.

Overall, Rahul Gandhi's efforts to rebuild the Congress Party have been significant. His leadership and advocacy have helped to promote a more united and inclusive political culture within the party, and have inspired many in India and around the world to work towards a more progressive and democratic political agenda.

# 8. The broader implications of Rahul Gandhi's political philosophy and vision

Rahul Gandhi's political philosophy and vision have significant implications not only for India, but for the broader global community as well. His commitment to social justice, economic equality, and environmental protection aligns with the values of many progressive movements around the world, and his advocacy for these values has the potential to inspire change beyond India's borders.

Rahul Gandhi's focus on empowering marginalized communities could be particularly influential in countries that struggle with issues of social and economic inequality. His emphasis on providing access to education, healthcare, and other resources for those who are most in need could serve as a model for governments and activists working to address similar issues in their own countries.

His commitment to democratic values and institutions is also significant, particularly at a time when many countries are facing challenges to their democratic systems. Rahul Gandhi's vocal opposition to authoritarianism and his advocacy for the protection of civil liberties and human rights could serve as an example for those who are fighting to defend democracy around the world.

Finally, Rahul Gandhi's focus on environmental protection could have global implications, particularly as the world faces increasing threats from climate change. His advocacy for sustainable development and his efforts to promote clean energy and reduce carbon emissions align with the goals of many international environmental organizations and could help to inspire greater action on this crucial issue.

Overall, Rahul Gandhi's political philosophy and vision have the potential to have significant implications beyond India's borders. His commitment to social justice, economic equality, environmental protection, and democratic values could serve as a model for governments and activists around the world who are working to build a better future for their communities and for the planet as a whole.

# VII. Conclusion

In conclusion, Rahul Gandhi has played a significant role in Indian politics as a leader within the Congress Party. His advocacy for social justice, economic equality, and environmental protection has earned him a significant following among those who share his vision for a more inclusive and progressive India.

Despite facing challenges such as electoral defeats, internal divisions within the party, and the perception of dynastic politics, Rahul Gandhi's commitment to these values remains steadfast. He has the potential to rebuild the Congress Party and to lead a more effective opposition to the policies of the ruling government, while also serving as a model for governments and activists around the world who are working towards a more just and equitable society.

Rahul Gandhi's political philosophy and vision have significant implications beyond India's borders, particularly in areas such as social and economic inequality, democracy, and environmental protection. As the world continues to grapple with these issues, Rahul Gandhi's leadership and advocacy could serve as a source of inspiration and hope for those who seek to build a better future for themselves and for future generations.

# 1. Summary of key themes and takeaways

● Rahul Gandhi is a prominent figure in Indian politics and a leader within the Congress Party.

● He is committed to social justice, economic equality, and environmental protection, and has advocated for the rights of marginalized communities.

● Despite facing challenges such as electoral defeats and internal divisions within the party, Rahul Gandhi's commitment to these values remains steadfast.

● He is a vocal critic of the ruling government's policies on a range of issues, including economic inequality, environmental degradation, and the erosion of civil liberties.

● Rahul Gandhi's political philosophy and vision have significant implications both for India and for the broader global community, particularly in areas such as social and economic inequality, democracy, and environmental protection.

● His leadership and advocacy could serve as a model for governments and activists around the world who are working towards a more just and equitable society.

# 2. Reflections on the significance of Rahul Gandhi for Indian politics

Rahul Gandhi's significance for Indian politics lies in his dedication to social justice, economic equality, and environmental protection. His commitment to these values provides a powerful foundation for his leadership within the Congress Party and his advocacy for a more inclusive and progressive India.

Despite facing numerous challenges and obstacles in his political career, Rahul Gandhi's continued efforts to promote these values have inspired many in India and around the world. His leadership and vision have helped to shape the political discourse in India and to promote a more just and equitable agenda for the country.

As India continues to grapple with issues of social and economic inequality, environmental degradation, and the erosion of democratic values, Rahul Gandhi's voice and advocacy will continue to be a significant force in Indian politics. His commitment to social justice and democratic ideals provides hope and inspiration for those who seek to build a better future for India and its people.

# 3. Possible future directions for research on Rahul Gandhi and his impact on Indian politics

Here are some possible future directions for research on Rahul Gandhi and his impact on Indian politics:

1. The role of identity politics in Rahul Gandhi's political career and its impact on his political philosophy and vision.
2. An analysis of the effectiveness of Rahul Gandhi's advocacy for social justice, economic equality, and environmental protection in driving policy change in India.
3. The impact of Rahul Gandhi's leadership and the Congress Party's policies on the lives of marginalized communities in India.
4. An examination of the role of social media in shaping public opinion about Rahul Gandhi and the Congress Party.
5. A comparative analysis of the leadership styles and policy positions of Rahul Gandhi and other prominent Indian politicians.

These are just a few possible areas of research that could contribute to a better understanding of Rahul Gandhi's impact on Indian politics. As Rahul Gandhi's political career continues to evolve, there will likely be many more opportunities to explore his leadership and advocacy for a more just and equitable India.

# About the Author

Instagram Id - swatantrabahadur15